LIVING WITH *Dementia*

LIVING WITH
Dementia

JO WEBB

Copyright © 2014 by Jo Webb.

Library of Congress Control Number: 2014911097
ISBN: Hardcover 978-1-4990-3879-8
Softcover 978-1-4990-3880-4
eBook 978-1-4990-3878-1

All rights reserved. No part of this book may be reproduced or transmitted in any form or by any means, electronic or mechanical, including photocopying, recording, or by any information storage and retrieval system, without permission in writing from the copyright owner.

Any people depicted in stock imagery provided by Thinkstock are models, and such images are being used for illustrative purposes only.
Certain stock imagery © Thinkstock.

This book was printed in the United States of America.

Rev. date: 06/18/2014

To order additional copies of this book, contact:
Xlibris LLC
1-888-795-4274
www.Xlibris.com
Orders@Xlibris.com
541763

I dedicate this Journal to my late husband,

Robert Lewis Conard.

May we meet in Heaven, and I will always love you.

"In sickness and in health till death do us part" has been in the marriage vows as long as I can remember. I don't remember attending a wedding where these words were not said by the minister and verbally agreed upon by the bride and groom. How many people have really thought about the meaning of these words and how they might affect you later in your marriage? How many couples think that it will be years before they have to face a health or death situation in their marriage? I didn't think that these words would come back to me numerous times in the 2 1/2 years of my second marriage. I met my husband on Classmates in the fall of 2008. We had dated in high school in the mid-1950s. Meanwhile, he had been in the Navy for four years, been married three times, and had recently lost his third wife. I had been married but divorced for over forty years in 2008. His wife had passed away the year before. When I saw his name on Classmates, I wrote him an email. I visited him several times in Arizona for several months in the winter of

2009. We fit together like a glove. We liked doing the same things, we each loved watching football, we both loved horses, and we talked every night on the phone for several hours. Our marriage in 2009 is the result of those emails and lengthy phone calls.

In the fall of 2010, the first signs of dementia were little things. He started getting lost in our home. He would start for the downstairs family room and think he had to go upstairs to get there. I would have to ask him where he was trying to go. I could not believe this was happening after we had been married a little over one year and four months. When I started seeing this sign and many other signs of dementia, I made a doctor appointment for him.

Doctor Paul Smith put him on an Alzheimer drug, Aricept, that was fairly new on the market. We saw almost immediate results. He seemed to feel better almost immediately and some of the signs of dementia were gone.

Living with someone you love, going into dementia, has been heart wrenching. He is now on two medications that are out for this horrible disease, Aricept and Namenda. His memory goes beyond getting lost in the house. I have asked him to bring a load of laundry down to the laundry room only to discover he was upstairs folding them. The mind gets so confused and a dementia patient has a very hard time following instructions. I have had to show him how to put a pillowcase on a pillow. These are all things we take for granted. How terrible it is for the patient not being able to remember. Yes, it is hard on the caregiver but at least they can still think for themselves. The patient knows that it is only going to get worse and eventually will not even know his wife. I don't look forward to that day. I do not know how I will handle it. When I discovered my husband on Classmates, I was so happy that I had someone to love and loved me, someone to travel with and enjoy taking trips together, someone who told me every day how much he loved me. That is what I will miss. I will miss him saying, "I love you so much".

At the present time, he is able to get through a day by himself. I am able to run out for short errands, we can pretend we are living a normal life that married couples take for granted.

However, we both know this is not the case for us. I have become not only a wife but also the mother to this person I love so much. I worry how I am going to be able to take care of him as this disease progresses. There will come a time that he will be incontinent and have to wear diapers, won't be able to feed or dress himself, and he will not be able to stay alone. Those are the problems ahead of me. I am living in another state other than my family so that will be a problem. I can foresee that we might have to move back to be with family for their help. When that time approaches, it will be me to do the packing, get rid of things, selling the house, and everything else that has to do with moving. I just hope I am able to hold it all together. One thing is for sure, I am not sorry we got married. He has given me the love that I looked for a long time. I will give him his dignity, my love, and whatever else it takes for him to live a comfortable life. He is my soul mate and me his. We discuss this illness of his, and we both know what end result will be.

01/02/2012:

I only wish I had dated each one of the above entries. So many things have changed with Bob's dementia. Within the last two weeks (Christmas holidays), Bob has gotten worse. We have been back from Ohio since 5:30 p.m. on Saturday, December 31, 2011. On the eve of our homecoming, Bob suddenly got up from the sofa, went to the dining room and said, "he would go to bed if he only knew where the bedroom was located". I took him by the hand and led him to the bedroom. I helped him undress and put on his new pajamas. I showed him where the bathroom was located and waited to say goodnight until he got back into bed. When he got into bed, I told him I would close up the house and come back to the bedroom to read so I could be near him. I actually broke down and cried while he held me in his arms. This was the first that I had broken down like this in front of him. He hugged me and kissed me and asked me not to cry. I kissed him good night and went back to the living room. I decided to turn off the television and lights and go back to the bedroom to read so I could lie beside him. The light does not bother him. When it was midnight (New Year's Day), I got up and gave him a kiss on the lips and forehead. This is so sad. So far, he knows who I am but when he loses that, what will I do? I dread that day.

01/02/2012:

This was another difficult day. Bob is not reading the paper anymore. When he talks, it is sometimes hard to understand him. And then he gets upset if he has to repeat what he said. He went to bed at 8:30 p.m. He said he was so tired.

01/03/2012:

Bob was asleep until 1:00 p.m. That means he slept for 16 hours. I had a hard time waking him up. I started trying to wake him up at 12:30 p.m., and it took me until 1:00 p.m. to get him out of bed. This is so stressful. I would not want my worst enemy to go through this dreadful disease with a loved one.

01/08/2012:

Today was a hard day to get through. First, I could not get Bob out of bed today. Finally, at 1:45 p.m., he got up. He had to be on a liquid diet today as he is getting a colonoscopy and endoscope test tomorrow morning. We have to be at the Surgery Center by 8:20 a.m. That is going to be difficult to get him up early in the morning. Bob started the day out by pouting that he had to be on the liquid diet. I could tell this was going to be a difficult day. Bob had to start on his taking the prep medicine at 5:00 p.m. He had to drink 8 oz. of the medicine every fifteen minutes. Then he had to drink two 8-ounce glasses of water. He did not complain much on that dosage. However, he had to repeat it at 8:00 p.m., and he did nothing but moan and talk about how sick it was making him. He did go through all the second dosage of medicine except for about 4 ounces of it. He just would not drink anymore. Men are such babies. No wonder they were not chosen to have the babies. They would never have been able to get through the labor part let alone the birthing process. He went to bed around 10:00 p.m. and so far is still asleep. I am worn out running back to the kitchen for the next dose of medicine. We set up camp in the master bath and bedroom. He was on the toilet from around 5:30 p.m. until 10:00 p.m. His butt must really hurt from sitting that long.

01/10/2012:

This is the day of Bob's upper and lower GI. I had to get up at 7:00 a.m. so I could have coffee and toast before I got Bob up so we could leave by 8:00 a.m. The test was scheduled at 8:20 a.m. Of course by the time Bob was processed and prepped, he was not taken back to surgery until around 10:45 a.m. He came through just fine. The nurse came and got me so the doctor could talk to both of us. The doctor said that Bob had no signs of a tumor or ulcers. His stomach was somewhat irritated and gave him a prescription for Zantac. Bob wanted to eat breakfast at iHop so we stopped there. The time was around 11:50 a.m. Bob ate a very good breakfast. He was somewhat confused at the Surgery Center. When I got him back home, he still experience the confusion. He has not been able to find any room he wants to go to and I have helped him get where he wants to go. This is really hard living with my loved one having this brain-starved order. It will eventually take away all of his memory where he will not even know who I am. It hurts now but it will get worse. I have already gone through this phase with my mother in her beginning stages of Alzheimer's dementia. I now understand why my father was so sad. He lived only six months after Mom was put in the nursing home. Dad died when he was only 76 years old, and Mom still lived in her locked up body and no memory in the nursing home in Athens, Ohio. Dad was living with my brother and his wife. No wonder Daddy was so upset. I had no idea until now what he must have been going through. I wish I could tell him how sorry I was for not being there all the time for him when he lost Mom. I was working in Milwaukee, WI, with my two daughters who were in grade school at the time. How lonely he must have felt when he went to visit her and she could not carry on a conversation and did not even know who he was. How that must hurt. And, this is what I will be experiencing in the future.

01/16/2012:

Bob had an appointment with our family physician, Dr. Paul Smith III. We discussed how his memory had done a downward spin since the week before Christmas while we were in Ohio. We discussed with Dr. Smith as to where he goes from here: does he get the brain scan that Dr. Birdwell suggested in his report, discussed about increasing his memory medicine, how many hours a day he is sleeping (12-14 hours a day), do we need to get a legal financial Power Of Attorney (POA), and his shortness of breath. Dr. Smith said he saw no need for an MRI of his brain that we knew he had dementia and why go through the expense of knowing what kind. He started Bob on an anti-depressant (same one that I take). I believe this is when the doctor increased the Aricept from 1 1/2 pills in the morning to 1 pill in the morning and one in the evening.

01/20/2012:

Back to see Dr. Smith as Bob is having some new symptoms he did not have on January 16, 2012. Bob is starting to have shortness of breath, hallucinations (started after taking the anti-depressant few days). The Doctor took him off the anti-depressant for two weeks and then go back on for four days in the evening and one pill starting on the fifth day. The Doctor checked and his lungs are not clear but his heart appears to be okay. Bob had a breathing treatment for his lungs. After we got home from the doctor, we came home and I fixed us an early dinner. Bob did not want to go downstairs to the family room so he stayed upstairs in the living room by himself. The television was broken but he didn't seem to mind. He started hallucinating again all evening. Bob does not carry on a conversation but instead rambles on and on. Sometimes he thinks he has something in his hand and tries brushing it off his hand. Earlier when I went upstairs to check on him, he said he was looking for Jo Ann (that is me). This is such a bad experience watching your loved one not understanding what is going on or who you are sometimes. Doctor Smith said that all dementia is the same and there is no actual difference. Bob seems better when he gets up in the morning/afternoon and then as the day goes into night, he starts having more memory problems.

06/15/2012:

Oh my goodness, time has flown, yet sometimes I do not feel that it has moved at all. I feel I am in a time warp and not made any progress. Bob has had numerous problems. So many things have happened between January 20, 2012 to the present date. I am going to attempt to update what has been happening. Bob went through a period when he slept until 1:00 to 2:00 PM. I just could not get him to get up from sleeping almost 15 hours. Bob had a Colonoscopy in January. The Doctor had to cut out couple of polyps. His Esophagus showed pre-cancer cells, but he would not have to go back for two years. Bob's memory loss is progressing very fast. Dr. Kundu, Neurologist, ordered an MRI for Bob and also a Brain Wave Test on February 8, 2012. Bob also had an appointment with Dr. Paul Smith, our family physician, for a follow-up for his cough and shortness of breath. His weight was 101 pounds. Another update is that Bob can still dress himself and feed himself. I do not let him cook however. On February 20, 2012,

Bob had his appointment with Dr.Kundu for the results of his MRI and Brain Scan. Dr. Kundu said the diagnosis is Alzheimer's dementia. I was so sad and upset. Bob didn't say anything, but I could see the disappointment on his face. Had the diagnosis been Vascular dementia, Bob had a better chance of getting better. Vascular dementia can be controlled by making certain changes in your lifestyle. Alzheimer's is a death sentence and Bob knows this.

Bob was admitted to the hospital on March 7, 2012 as he was just out-of-it since he had taken the drug "Senoquil" prescribed by Dr. Kundu. Stephanie and Samantha were here helping me clear out the garage the entire week. Stephanie thought we should have Bob taken to the local hospital. After numerous tests, the results were he had low blood sugar, low potassium, dehydration, low phosphorus, and an Urinary Tract Infection. He was in the hospital until March 13, 2012. I inquired about receiving at home health care so it was arranged with Bradley Health Care. While in the hospital, I got a call from Dr. Smith's office that the Simvastatin 80mg was recalled and lowered to 40mg. However, the hospital doctor discontinued this drug.

07/31/2012:

So much has happened since my last writings. Bob was taken to the Hospital as I said above and was allowed to come home on March 13, 2012. He was getting along pretty good, able to walk and talk, and all normal stuff. Then on May 27, 2012, I called 911 as he had not been eating or drinking any fluids last couple of days. I knew he was getting dehydrated again. He was admitted to the hospital and stayed there until May 30, 2012. Around 6:00 p.m., he was moved to Signature Health Care for physical therapy.

Bob stayed at Signature Health Care for the full 30 days. The night before he was to come home, the nursing home called to tell me they had called an ambulance, and that he was very sick. They did not say how he was sick but very sick. On July 29, 2012, he very clearly said the word Momma. His eyes were open but he was not looking at anyone.

8/01/2012:

Bob has been asleep since Monday afternoon, July 30. His eyes are open sometimes. He is in a little pain. The Hospice nurse said to give him the Morphine if he starts to moan. He never really opened his eyes until this morning when Jay was giving him his bath. He was very constipated and the Hospice nurse had to clean him out, and it was very painful for him. I have been so lucky to have Hospice Care. There are some things I just could not do. They are all so nice to Bob. They talk to him and sooth him. He has had no food or water since early Monday morning. They told me that he does not have much time left, and that he could pass away in the next couple of days. I listen to them tell me this, but my mind is not registering what they are saying. I am missing my soul mate already. He always told me every day he loved me and how lucky he was to have found me (I found him but that's okay). The last 8 months have been tough on both of us. He was able to get around the house with my help in guiding him where he wanted to go.

I often wonder, had we not gone to Ohio over the Christmas holidays, would he have gone downhill as fast as he did? I will never know, and I do realize I cannot blame myself, but I so wish he was sitting with me in the living room.

08/02/2012:

My daughters had been planning to come down to see us and give me some help with Bob for the last few weeks. They arrived around 12:15 a.m., and Bob was in his bed with his eyes shut. The girls had worked all day and then driven all evening to get down here. We sat and talked for a while for them to unwind from the day of working and traveling. We decided it was time for bed. I went through the living room to give him my goodnight kiss. Bob's eyes were open, and I called for the girls to come in to see him. He looked at Stephanie and then Jen and me. He took three short breaths and one long one, and then he was gone. I was so shocked as I was not expecting him to pass away that quickly.

The days following Bob's death are somewhat of a blur to me. Stephanie and Jennifer stayed until Monday afternoon and then headed back to Ohio. Stephanie came into the family room and said, "Now that we kept you busy all weekend, after we leave, you are going to sit down and bawl your eyes out. You need to let go and just cry and cleanse your soul". I did not think she knew what she was talking about; however, they had not been gone for very long when I suddenly realized I was all alone again and would never see Bob again. It had not hit me until at that very time that he was gone. I had been just getting through each day by osmosis. I got up every day around 9:00 a.m., drank coffee, ate a piece of toast, and started the day. In the beginning, I took care of Bob first and changed him into clean clothes, fed him since he could not feed himself, and then fed the dogs and cats, and finally I took care of me.

12/23/2012:

Well, much has happened since Bob passed away. I am now living in my old house in Dayton, Ohio. The girls convinced me I should move back to Ohio. I moved sooner than I had planned on November 10, 2012. Stephanie came down for five days early November. She went with me to put the house up for sale, to trade in both cars for one car. I called the movers and arranged for them to come on Friday, November 8, to pack what was left and then to move me on Saturday, November 9. They drove half way to Ohio and arrived on Sunday morning, November 10. The move was very hard on me. I really did not want to leave my house in Cleveland, TN, but I had no choice. My surgeon had told me in October that I needed to have back surgery within 4-6 weeks. That I would be in a nursing home for 100 days and have to wear a brace. My daughters and I decided if I had to have it, I should be back in Ohio where my family is located. I would have lots of help. I went to see a second surgeon here in Dayton only to find out I did not need surgery. What a relief that is to me.

I miss Bob so much. If I can start to feeling better, I plan to volunteer at the Alzheimer Association. I want to give back for the care that Bob received.

Jo Webb was born in Hillsboro, Ohio, and left there at the age of ten when her father was transferred to Wilmington, Ohio. She lived there for twenty years. During that time, she was married, had children, and was divorced at age twenty-nine. She had two daughters to support. Luckily, she worked for the Federal Government and was able to live on her own.

She worked for twenty-eight years for the Federal Government and for seventeen years at a local television station in Dayton, Ohio. She is the mother of two daughters, four granddaughters, and four great-granddaughters and her close companion Chase, a Bichon Frise. Part of her Government career was spent in Milwaukee, WI. While there, she was promoted to work in the Procurement Office as a Procurement Clerk. She had found her niche and was extremely successful in this field. She was promoted to the position of Chief of Procurement Office and was presented with many awards. She transferred to Wright-Patterson Air Force Base to work in their Procurement Office and the name had been changed to Contracting Center. Within a year, she was promoted to a supervisory position. She retired in 1987 at the age of 47. Her second career was in a local television station. This turned out to be her fun job without all the pressures and long hours at her prior job. At the age of 68 years old, she retired from there.

She comes from a family of teachers, artists, and writers. When she re-married in June 2009 to a former classmate of hers, they planned to live a full life together and do lots of traveling.

Her husband started having memory problems in the fall of 2010. He was given the drug, Aricept. After several months, his condition worsened and another medicine, Namenda, was prescribed to go along with Aricept.

This journal starts with his condition starting in December 2011 and ultimately his untimely death in 2012. She wanted to explain to current and future caregivers what it is like to take care of an Alzheimer's patient, who is also your spouse.

Synopsis

"Living with Dementia" is a caregiver's first-hand involvement caring for her husband of only two and half years diagnosed with Alzheimer's Dementia early in their marriage. This journal gives people, who are also Caregivers of a loved one, what to expect plus one's feelings during the illness until their loved one passes away.